The Social Licence to Operate

Your Management Framework for Complex Times

Leeora Black

Australian Centre for Corporate Social Responsibility

leeorablack@accsr.com.au

Routledge
Taylor & Francis Group

LONDON AND NEW YORK

First published 2013 by Greenleaf Publishing Limited

Published 2017 by Routledge
2 Park Square, Milton Park, Abingdon, Oxon OX14 4RN
711 Third Avenue, New York, NY 10017, USA

Routledge is an imprint of the Taylor & Francis Group, an informa business

ISBN 978-1-909293-72-4 (pbk)

A catalogue record for this title is available from the British Library.

Page design and typesetting by Alison Rayner
Cover by Becky Chilcott

Abstract

THE SOCIAL LICENCE TO OPERATE began as a metaphor to bring attention to the need for companies to earn acceptance from their host communities. Today, it is a management framework for complex times.

This book aims to provide a road map for companies to work with their stakeholders to create a foundation for truly sustainable community development.

It contains a framework for managing your social licence, tools, and case studies. It will help you develop a social licence strategy, which is essentially a stakeholder engagement strategy for organisations to navigate complex socio-political environments.

This book is for managers in any company facing rising social scrutiny due to unwanted social or environmental impacts. You may be working in natural resources, renewable energy, oil and gas, forestry, construction, manufacturing, retail, food processing, pharmaceuticals or any industry that is facing rising stakeholder expectations and increasing criticism.
....

About the Author

 **DR LEEORA BLACK** is Managing Director of the Australian Centre for Corporate Social Responsibility, a specialist management consulting and training firm based in Melbourne, Australia. After a career in corporate communications and consulting, she completed a doctorate in corporate social responsibility at Monash University. She is a globally recognised authority on social responsibility, stakeholder engagement and the social licence to operate, advising global companies, government-owned corporations and civic sector organisations on how to develop collaborative relationships that contribute to sustainable community development.

Acknowledgments

I AM INDEBTED to my colleague of more than a decade, Robert Boutilier, PhD. His pioneering work on the social licence to operate, together with Ian Thomson, PhD, forms the inspiration for this book.

I am also grateful to my team at the Australian Centre for Corporate Social Responsibility (ACCSR), who have worked with me over the years in the development and application of the social licence to operate.

Finally, this book would not be possible without the opportunity to work with the pioneering companies who engaged ACCSR in projects to apply the social licence framework described in this book.

Dedication

To my husband, Bob Kochen.

Contents

Abstract...5

About the Author 7

Acknowledgments...9

Dedication...11

Introduction..15

1 From Metaphor to
    Management Approach....................................17
    Defining the social licence...............................17
    Levels of the social licence 18
    Four building blocks of your social licence 21

2 The Business Case for
    the Social Licence..31
    Socio-political risk 32
    Post-materialist values and NGOs...................35

3 Stakeholder Networks and Stakeholder
    Engagement Capabilities 39
    Mapping your stakeholder network...................39
    Stakeholder network patterns 42

Stakeholder engagement capabilities..........................48

4 Measuring the Social Licence............................51
   Measuring perceptions 51
   When to measure and how to chart results 56
   Combining social licence and
   stakeholder network insights.............................58

5 Developing a Social Licence Strategy...........63
   How to identify stakeholders.............................63
   Understand the issues..66
   Conduct a social licence evaluation.............................68
   Choose tactics to build your social licence.................71
   Case studies on social licence strategy.......................75

6 Using International Frameworks for
   Your Social Licence 81
   Social licence assessment and strategy.....................83
   Reporting your social licence 92

7 Conclusion...95

   Notes 97

Introduction

'WE'VE STOPPED ONE COAL MINE from going ahead and we can do it again.' The voice at the other end of the phone was calm and clear. It was 2010 and I was working for a group of coal miners that collectively operated 18 mines in the Upper Hunter region of New South Wales, about three hours' drive north-west of Sydney. The caller was referring to community opposition to the Bickham Coal Mine, which months earlier had been refused a permit by the NSW government – the first coal mine ever knocked back in a State heavily dependent on coal exports.[1]

The coal miners needed to rebuild their social licence. Although they collectively employed around 12,000 people in a regional population of less than 40,000, community acceptance was at rock-bottom.

The dilemma faced by the Upper Hunter coal miners is familiar in many industries. Communities simply don't want you operating in their neighbourhood. They may be concerned about quality of life impacts, health, access to services, pollution, employment, local economic impacts, visual amenity or loss of natural resources as a result of your operations. Communities know your operations will bring benefits, but increasingly, they are saying the benefits are not worth the costs. Even if you have all the legal permits, communities refuse to grant your social licence to operate.

This book is about how to build and maintain your company's social licence to operate. Not with the traditional tools of communications and persuasion campaigns, and not by sponsorship and donations, but by working collaboratively with communities to make a real and enduring contribution to sustainable development. It contains a framework for managing your social licence, tools, case studies and helpful tips. It provides advice on how to develop a social licence strategy, which is essentially a stakeholder engagement strategy for organisations to navigate complex socio-political environments.

This book is for managers in any company facing rising social scrutiny due to unwanted social or environmental impacts. You may be working in natural resources, renewable energy, oil and gas, forestry, construction, manufacturing, retail, food processing, pharmaceuticals or a host of other industries that are experiencing rising stakeholder expectations and increasing criticism.

This book can also be used by communities who want to benefit from these companies' presence in their communities while preserving the qualities of life they hold dear. The aim of this book is to provide a road map for companies to work together with their stakeholders to create a foundation for truly sustainable community development.

....

CHAPTER 1

From Metaphor to Management Approach

IT'S EASY TO SEE when you've lost your social licence. Demonstrations, blockades, negative publicity, complaints, sometimes even violence against your company's property or people, are typical signs that you've lost it. It's harder to know when you've got it, or how to build it. In this chapter I define the social licence to operate and describe its basic building blocks. These building blocks form a management framework that you can use to measure, analyse and develop an enduring social licence for your company, operation or project.

Defining the social licence

The social licence to operate began as a metaphor comparing the ability of communities to stop mining projects with the ability of governments to do the same. It was coined by Jim Cooney, a former executive with the international gold miner, Placer Dome. He used the phrase in a meeting with the World Bank in 1997 and it gained wider currency at a World Bank sponsored meeting on mining and the community later that year. Others developed the concept based on their experiences consulting with companies that had lost, or were about to lose, their social licences.[2]

The social licence to operate is not a piece of paper or a document like a government licence. It's a form of social acceptance or approval that companies or projects earn through consistent and trustworthy behaviour and interactions with their stakeholders. It's a socially constructed perception that your company or project has a legitimate place in the community. It is built on effective stakeholder engagement; the processes your organisation uses to involve people in decisions that affect them.

Like reputation, the social licence is hard to earn and easy to lose. But it's not the same as reputation. Your reputation is the outcome of how much people like your company based on their own experiences and what they hear or read about you. Your social licence is the judgement by communities about whether your company is a proper and fitting entity that deserves to be part of their community. It's a judgement about the legitimacy of your company or operations.

Put simply, the social licence is the level of acceptance or approval continually granted to an organisation's operations or project by local community and other stakeholders.

Levels of the social licence

Your social licence can rise or fall in response to your actions or the actions of others. This suggests the social licence has levels. Our work shows that that there are four levels of the social licence, which range from lowest to highest: withdrawal, acceptance, approval and psychological identification. It can vary across time or between stakeholder groups in response to actions by the company and/or its stakeholders (see Figure 1).

....

FIGURE 1. Four levels of the social licence, showing the conditions for moving from one level to another.

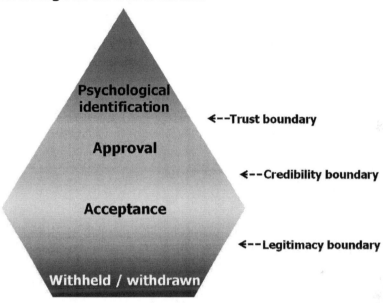

Reproduced with permission of Robert Boutilier, PhD.

....

At the lowest level, you don't have a social licence. It's withdrawn. You may experience negative publicity, demonstrations and blockades, or even violence against your property or people. You need to establish legitimacy as a condition to move to the acceptance level.

It's easy to confuse silence with acceptance, and acceptance with approval. When communities accept your operations, they listen to you, they may occasionally express misgivings or complain, but mostly, they hope their concerns will be addressed and generally give you the benefit of the doubt.

To move to the approval level, you need to establish credibility. You can earn credibility by displaying consistently trustworthy behaviour, listening, keeping promises and fair dealing. At the approval level you have stakeholder support for your project.

If you can earn the full trust of stakeholders, your project's social licence can rise to the level of psychological identification. At this level the community sees its future as tied to the future of your project or company. Your company and the community share goals, interests and benefits. Communities are willing to fight for your interests because they share those interests.

Most companies or projects are in the acceptance or approval range most of the time. The psychological identification level is rare and may take decades to evolve. Most importantly, the social licence can rise and fall in response to your actions, and the actions of others in the community or stakeholder network.

Who is a stakeholder?

Stakeholders become stakeholders because they have a stake in, or an interest in, or are affected by, or can influence, an issue that brings them into relationship with a given organisation. They get organised around these issues because together, they have more power. They may form new organisations or join existing ones. Your social licence is granted by your stakeholders.

Four building blocks of your social licence

The social licence also has four components, superimposed on the levels (see Figure 2). These are the building blocks of the social licence, and provide your road map for building your company's social licence. The building blocks are: legitimate benefits; social capital; the social contract; and institutionalised trust. The foundation is legitimate benefits. You can think of the building blocks as strategies for developing or improving your social licence.

....

FIGURE 2. Four components of the social licence to operate.

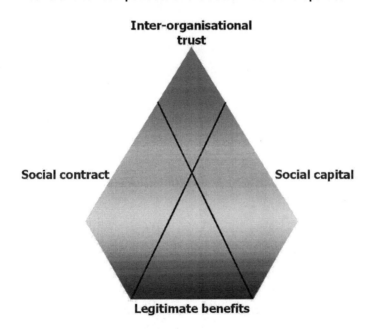

**Inter-organisational
trust**

Social contract

Social capital

Legitimate benefits

Reproduced with permission of Robert Boutilier, PhD.

....

Legitimate benefits

At the most basic level you need to provide legitimate benefits to communities. Stakeholders need to see that they can benefit from a company's presence or project in a meaningful way. Benefits like bringing new jobs to a region or donations to local groups are often cited by companies as if this were enough to establish a social licence.

It's not.

Benefits can include things like local purchasing, strategic community investment, local sponsorships, educational or health programs, community capacity building initiatives, and involvement in local community, environmental, cultural or sporting organisations. The benefits should be relevant to the needs of a particular community and seen by the community as legitimate and not tokenistic.

A strategy of providing legitimate benefits could help you achieve an acceptance level of the social licence, as indicated in Figure 2. But your social licence will be vulnerable. If the benefits finish, or if stakeholder expectations of benefits change, your social licence will drop. Communities can develop an unhealthy dependence on your organisation if this is the only social licence strategy you ever use.

To establish a more stable and enduring social licence you need to build social capital in your company's stakeholder relationships and play your part in ensuring a durable social contract in the region affected by your company's operations. These two strategies should be pursued together, with the relative emphasis given to each strategy depending on the results of your social licence evaluation (see Conduct a Social Licence Evaluation, in Chapter 5: Developing a social Licence Strategy).

Social capital

Management experts Don Cohen and Laurence Prusak laid out the role that social capital plays inside organisations in their groundbreaking book *In Good Company: How Social Capital Makes Organizations Work* (2001). They described it as '. . . the stock of active connections among people: the trust, mutual understanding and shared values and behaviors that bind the members of human networks and communities and make cooperative action possible'. The concept can also be applied to relationships between companies and their stakeholders.

Management theorists Adler and Kwon[3] said social capital is derived from the idea of goodwill and described it as an asset from which benefits can flow, benefits like the ability of people to cooperate with one another in pursuit of shared goals.

Social capital is an attribute of relationship quality that when present in high amounts, enables co-operation and collaboration towards shared goals. Company–stakeholder relationships that are high in social capital can allow them to work together towards the goal of sustainable community development. To build collaborative relationships, trust is essential.

Companies can earn trust in their day-to-day relationships with stake-holders by consistent and ethical behaviour; by keeping promises, and by listening carefully to stakeholders.

Starting to see how stakeholder engagement is the basis for earning your social licence to operate?

Social contract

The social contract strategy is more oriented towards issues of perceived fairness and the welfare of the broader region in which you operate. It is based on the idea of the social contract; in this case an implicit agreement between corporations and communities about the right of a company to operate within a community and the conditions under which it is accepted.[4] The social contract component of the social licence to operate is the cornerstone of long-term legitimacy of your operation or company. Stakeholders develop feelings about the fairness of the costs and benefits your company brings to the whole region. This can be especially challenging when your operation is part of an extended global supply chain, where the benefits of your company are widespread and distant, but the costs are borne by local communities. Think of factory workers in Bangladesh or Guatemala producing garments for global retailers or mine workers in central Africa digging metals for iPods.

The key to success in building the social contract element of the social licence often lies in participation in regional economic development initiatives or other programs that contribute to the well-being of the broader region. In this way companies can learn about local ways of doing things and demonstrate respect for local priorities.

Multi-stakeholder engagement is the key process through which the social contract element of the social licence can be earned. Multi-stakeholder engagement can help companies and communities form a shared view of what is important for a sustainable future for the region and provides opportunities to build social capital directly with key stakeholder organisations. You can read case studies of multi-stakeholder engagement in Chapter 5: Developing a Social Licence Strategy.

Institutionalised trust

Institutionalised trust is not so much a specific strategy as an outcome of the previous three strategies, executed well. When a company is effectively building relationships with stakeholders (social capital), and playing a meaningful role in sustainability of the broader region, it can eventually develop institutionalised trust, a form of taken-for-grantedness or strong psychological identification whereby the community feels a sense of 'ownership' of the project. At this point stakeholders would agree, based on their history of relations with your company, that you are genuinely concerned about the community's best interests, and that you support those who you negatively affect, that you take the community's interests into account and involve the community or stakeholders in decisions that affect them.

In other words, your stakeholder engagement has been exemplary and you are an outstanding corporate citizen. This level of social licence is rare. It is also not always the optimal level of social licence, as it can be accompanied by dependence on your company. The anguish experienced by communities when longstanding companies need to close an operation is evidence of this.

The four components are not always completely distinct and separate strategies. You may pursue a strategy that has elements of all. Further, a given set of tactics can work to build each of these components of the social licence, given different contexts. For example, an action like promoting education might be considered a legitimate benefit if you endow a chair at a local university. Consulting local schools to find out what they need to get better student outcomes might boost social capital in your relationships with the schools. If you participate in a multi-stakeholder partnership with education providers, government, business and social sector organisations to build a new innovation precinct in your area, you are making a contribution to the well-being of the broader region and helping secure your social contract. And after many years, if the innovation precinct comes to be associated with your organisation's name, this could indicate you have institutionalised trust, the highest level of the social licence.

> ### SLO levels and natural resource development
> Among the most common situations where companies need a social licence strategy is for the development of natural resources, whether they are fossil fuel-based, like minerals, oil and gas, or whether they are renewable, like wind. Different components of the social licence can be targeted at each stage to build community acceptance of your project and contribute to sustainable community development. These tips are equally relevant whether you are operating in a remote or populous area, or a developing or first world country.

TABLE 1. Components of the social licence at different stages of natural resource development

Natural resource development stage	Legitimate benefits	Social capital	Social contract	Institutionalised trust	Sample activities for earning your social licence to operate
Exploration	✓	✓			• Understand the social, cultural and economic context for your proposed development. • Develop good relationships with community leaders and organisations. • Involve community leaders in identification of ways your proposed project can bring local benefits. • Involve community leaders in the development and implementation of your community relations plan for all stages of the development, including exploration. • Take social licence baseline measures against which progress can be measured in future.

27

Natural resource development stage	Legiti-mate benefits	Social capital	Social contract	Insti-tution-alised trust	Sample activities for earning your social licence to operate
Development and construction	✓	✓	✓		• Hire and buy locally to the greatest extent possible. • Ensure contractor and temporary workforces adhere to your code of conduct with respectful behaviour both on and off the job. • If temporary workers' camps are required consult and collaborate with local organisations and authorities on the location and conditions. • Maintain good relationships with community leaders and organisations and provide regular updates on your progress. • Monitor your social licence and understand the issues that need attention to maintain or build it.
Operations	✓	✓	✓	✓	• Hire and buy locally to the greatest extent possible. • Develop and implement capacity building programs to ensure the community can take advantage of your employment and procurement opportunities. • Become involved in the local community through participation in civic, cultural, educational or environmental initiatives. • Support the development of other industries that can fill an employment gap when you leave. • Monitor your social licence and understand the issues that need attention to maintain or build it.

THE SOCIAL LICENCE TO OPERATE:
YOUR MANAGEMENT FRAMEWORK FOR COMPLEX TIMES

Natural resource development stage	Legitimate benefits	Social capital	Social contract	Institutionalised trust	Sample activities for earning your social licence to operate
Decommissioning and closure	✓	✓	✓	✓	• Rehabilitate natural landscapes consistent with the community's vision for its future. • Consider what public infrastructure can be left for public benefit and how it will be maintained (e.g. will you establish a trust fund for ongoing maintenance or other future benefits?). • Work with other industries to help them adapt to a future without you, e.g. by building workforce capabilities or providing training for your workers to do other jobs. • Leave the place in as good or better condition as you found it.

CHAPTER 2

The Business Case for the Social Licence

THE BUSINESS CASE FOR MANAGING your social licence is all about managing risk. Managing risk (and its corollary, managing reputation) is the most common reason that companies begin to think about how to protect their social licence.

To protect a social licence, a company needs to play a constructive role in sustainable community development. The International Guidance Standard on Social Responsibility, ISO 26000, puts the case for sustainable community development at least in part as reinforcing and protecting democratic and civic values. This suggests that a social licence may afford some protection against political instability.

Businesses that have big impacts on communities and their quality of life increasingly recognise that there is both an ethical imperative and a sound business case for focusing on sustainable community development. Such business may be:

- Big employers (retailers and manufacturers)

- Have a pervasive influence on society and the economy (banks, utilities, pharmaceutical companies and telcos), or

- Make a big environmental impact (mining, oil and gas and construction).

The type of risks that a social licence can help you manage are those risks arising from the interaction of social and political factors; that is, socio-political risk.

Socio-political risk

Corporations face both social risk and political risks. Put them together and you can find yourself dealing with threats to your company's very legitimacy.

Social risk arises from the impact of your operations on social issues. The impact of social risk on companies is well illustrated by the story of Nike. For 20 years Nike endured activist campaigns to improve workers' conditions at its suppliers' factories. The campaign led to boycotts, strikes and lawsuits that trashed the company's reputation and ultimately led to profound changes in the way Nike does business. Changes rippled across the entire footwear and apparel industry although there is still a long way to go (one only has to think of the tragic Rana Plaza factory collapse in Bangladesh in April 2013).

Any number of stakeholders may transmit a social risk to various divisions in a company.[5] Investors can bring shareholder resolutions; customers can demand changes in a company's supply chain policies; trade unions may raise concerns about outsourcing of jobs overseas.

Social risks gain an added element of political risk when stakeholders, including NGOs and activists, attempt to influence the distribution of rights and responsibilities, and their associated costs and benefits, among community members or stakeholders.[6]

Why do stakeholders act?

To become active, stakeholders must:

- recognise a problem;

- believe they can do something about it; and

- expect they can get a worthwhile outcome.

NGO campaigns

Socio-political risks occur when stakeholders, sometimes acting alone and sometimes acting in coalitions, attempt to change the amount of responsibility you take for the impact of your operations. Campaigns run by sophisticated NGOs are good examples of how socio-political risk is introduced to companies, although socio-political risk also arises from grassroots campaigns like the 'Lock the Gate' in Australia,[7] an alliance of over 160 community and environment groups that opposes 'inappropriate mining'.

For example, Greenpeace ran a gruesome campaign against Nestle in 2010 to stop it buying palm oil from companies that destroy orang-utan habitat, with a spoof on its 'Have a Break, Have a Kit Kat' advertisement. The spoof showed an office worker snacking on bleeding orang-utan fingers that he produced from inside a Kit Kat wrapper. As a result of this campaign, Nestle suspended contracts with its palm oil supplier Sinar Mas. Sinar Mars went on to work with the environmental group The Forest Trust on a Forest Conservation Policy, and 18 months later, Nestle resumed its purchases of palm oil.

Greenpeace had effectively challenged Nestle's social licence to operate, at least in regards to its iconic Kit Kat brand, although the risk to Sinar Mars was much more profound, with both sales and share price affected. The campaign worked. Greenpeace was able to force a change in the amount of responsibility both Nestle and Sinar Mars accepted for the impacts of their operations on nature and animals.

Sometimes, stakeholders want you to accept more responsibility for your impacts, as in the Greenpeace Kit Kat campaign. Sometimes, they just want to stop you. For example, a coalition of groups,[8] including Greenpeace, the New York-based Rockefeller Family Fund, the Australia Institute, Lock the Gate and the Environmental Defenders Office launched a fundraising prospectus in 2012 aiming to raise nearly $6 million for a campaign called 'Stopping the Australian Coal Export Boom'.

The prospectus said: 'The first priority is to get in front of the critical projects to slow them down in the approval process. This means lodging legal challenges to five new coal port expansions, two major rail lines and up to a dozen of the key mines.'

At this scale, a group of activists was challenging the entire coal mining industry's social licence. The proposed campaign also illustrates how easily a threat to the social licence can transform into costly conflicts. One recent study estimated the cost of conflict between communities and mining companies at up to $20 million per week if production is delayed.[9]

Socio-political sustainability

The inverse of socio-political risk is socio-political sustainability. As aptly described by my colleague, Robert Boutilier:[10]

Socio-political sustainability means going beyond teaching a man to fish so he can feed himself and sell fish to the company cafeteria. It means helping his fisherman's organisation and the municipal government rid their social network structure of its dysfunctional configurations so they can collaborate widely to set up a regional fish market and establish links with international fish buyers.

That sounds like sustainable community development and is how a social licence looks when it is well established.

Post-materialist values and NGOs

I'm often asked why the social licence concept is emerging now and why activists seem to be so much more demanding than they used to be. The answer lies in changing social values and the simultaneous growth of the global civic sector over the past 20 years.

The political scientist Ronald Inglehart explains this trend.[11] He shows how long periods of economic prosperity, such as the Western world has known since the 1950s, lead to the spread of post-materialist values. Post-materialist values are the things we tend focus on after our basic material needs for food, housing and work are satisfied. They are things like freedom of expression, autonomy, gender equality and environmental preservation. Young people tend to embrace these values more readily than older people, and as they grow older, post-materialist values become more widespread in society. These changing values have been charted since 1990 by the World Values Survey (see **www.worldvaluessurvey.com**).

Post-materialist values find ready expression in social movements and the civic sector organisations that emerge to fight for social or environmental causes. Social movements are not alone in embracing most materialist values. The commitment of so many companies around the world to sustainable development and corporate social responsibility is evidence of that.

But social movements act like a weathervane for where sentiment is trending on major social and environmental issues. Environmental groups, community health groups, neighbourhood groups, unions and rights advocacy groups can all become active on issues that affect a company's social licence.

The civic sector is also bigger than it used to be. Its growth far outpaced the growth of the private sector. For example, from 1994 to 2004, the United States gross domestic product grew by an inflation-adjusted 36%. The revenues of the non-profit sector, however, grew 61.5% in the same period and its assets grew by 90.7%.[12]

It's now easier than ever for any company to come under scrutiny and potential threats to its social licence. Evaluation and management of socio-political risk should be on the agenda of every company, particularly those with far-reaching social, environmental and economic impacts.

The business case for building a social licence to operate

- Reduce risks to your operations from social issues
  - A high level of social licence is the result of effectively understanding and responding to social issues. The higher the level of social licence, the lower the level of risk.

- Avoid being targeted by NGO campaigns

  - NGO campaigns, especially international campaigns, can get traction at a local level when local stakeholders feel like their needs and values are not being addressed by your operations. Joining up with international NGOs gives local stakeholders more power to get their issues addressed by your organisation.

  - Instead of being targeted by NGOs, seek collaboration with NGOs to help you address the issues that are most important to your local stakeholders.

- Insure against costly delays to important projects

  - Loss of your social licence can lead to demonstrations, boycotts, road blocks and delays. The cost of such delays is inevitably much higher than the cost of your social licence strategy.

- Enjoy peaceful and collaborative relationships with your stakeholders

  - Collaborative relationships are the basis for being able to address shared goals or solve shared problems.

- Get a better return on community investment programs

  - When you know what the real needs and issues of the community are you can ensure you are investing in the things that really matter.

- Become a valued member of the community and improve your reputation

  - There is a high correlation between a good reputation and a high social licence. Social licence strategies create opportunities to work together with local communities on issues that are important to them. Your positive role in the community will create trust and good word-of-mouth, which translates into positive regard for your organisation.

CHAPTER 3

Stakeholder Networks and Stakeholder Engagement Capabilities

STAKEHOLDERS HAVE RELATIONSHIPS with one another, as well as with your organisation. The network of relationships between your stakeholders forms the context within which your social licence is issued. This is your stakeholder *network*. Only your stakeholder network is capable of issuing a valid and durable social licence. Stable stakeholder networks produce durable social licences.

A company that wants to restore, earn, maintain or improve its social licence has to first understand the network structure of its communities. Who are the stakeholders? What are their interests and needs? Do they see eye to eye on issues of importance or are they divided?

These fundamental questions need answers to be able to develop a social licence strategy. A stakeholder network map is therefore an essential tool for developing a road map to build your social licence.

Mapping your stakeholder network

A stakeholder network map can show you which organisations can work effectively together on important issues in the community, and where there are conflicts or gaps that if addressed, could strengthen your stakeholder network.

Social network analysis software can plot these relationships systematically. But if you don't have access to that, you can use a freehand method I use in my stakeholder engagement master class workshops. Start with a small group of stakeholders, as the exercise can quickly become complicated.

First, identify a group of stakeholders that has an interest in an issue that is important to your organisation (see How to identify stakeholders). For the sake of the exercise, let's say they all have an interest in biodiversity preservation in the area where you are operating.

Then, put the names of the stakeholder in a circle, as in Figure 3. Thinking about which stakeholders are capable of working together effectively on the issue, draw lines to connect those who can work well together on the issue. Count the number of connections each stakeholder has with the other stakeholders in the network. The stakeholders with the highest number of connections to others are likely to be the most influential.

In Figure 3, there are two equally well-connected stakeholders, G and D. Now consider that stakeholder D grants your organisation a low level of social licence but stakeholder G grants you a high level. Notice that they are not connected to one another, and they have different relationships with others in the network. But some of stakeholder D's stakeholders could work with stakeholder G. Stakeholder D can work well with A and B. Can you see how to build your organisation's social licence in the network depicted in Figure 3?

....

FIGURE 3. Free-hand stakeholder network mapping.

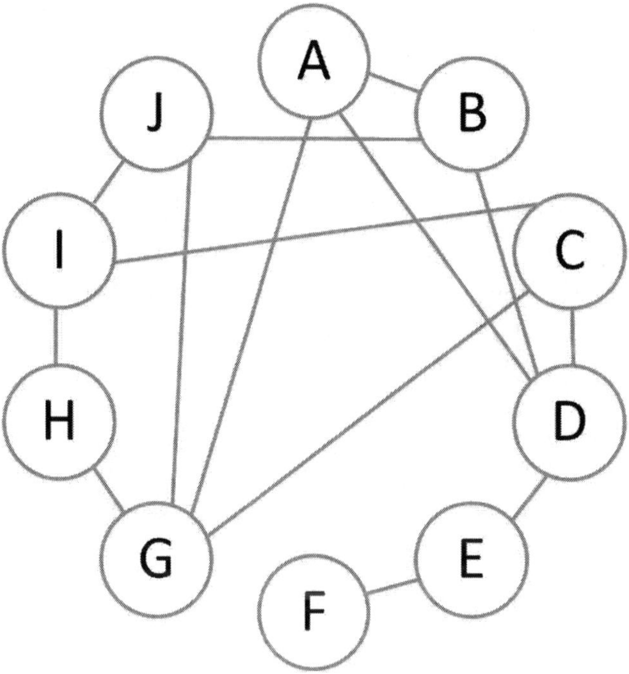

....

There are some options. You could invite G, A and C to a meeting to discuss possible solutions to biodiversity problems. G gives you a high social licence, so A and C might, too. And they can both work with D. You could then ask A and C to find out if D would like to get involved. Together, D and G could get all the stakeholders working together on the issue. If you can develop a biodiversity conservation program that appeals to both G and D, you may be able to lift your social licence through the whole stakeholder network.

Stakeholder network patterns

Different types of stakeholder network patterns are more, or less, capable of issuing a valid and durable social licence. The validity of the social licence depends on the inclusiveness of decision-making. The durability of the social licence depends on the accountability of leaders to the community and the community's ability to adapt to inevitable change.

A matrix of hypothetical stakeholder network patterns were developed by my colleague, Dr Robert Boutilier, based on two different types of social capital, bonding and bridging. We have found several of them in social licence evaluations we have undertaken (see Figure 4).

Two types of social capital

Bonding social capital can be thought of as the strength of trust and shared values within a group. It creates strong loyalty within groups. Bonding social capital was put to good use by Grameen Bank which recognised that the loyalty of village women to one another meant that micro-credit initiatives would work.

Grameen started by lending small amounts to women in small groups who share the same background and high trust. The money helped the women start small businesses and break the cycle of poverty. The initiative works because of bonding social capital: none of the women would want to let their friends down by defaulting on a loan.

A high level of bonding social capital is not always good. The Ku Klux Klan and the mafia have high bonding social capital.

Bridging social capital can be thought of as relationships between groups that are different from one another. It helps groups and people extend their networks to find others who can help them solve shared problems. Without bridging social capital in a community, a company may not be able to develop the 'social contract' element of the social licence as they would find it difficult to establish good relationships with different groups in the community.

Many writers have suggested that bonding social capital must be developed before bridging capital can exist. Both types are important in stakeholder networks that are most capable of issuing a valid and durable social licence. For example, a group of schools might enter a partnership with a group of companies to develop work-readiness traineeship program. For this to work, the schools need to have some social capital among themselves and the companies need some social capital among themselves. This enables them to see eye to eye on the issues that lead to establishment of a traineeship program. Bridging social capital enables the traineeship program to be developed.

See the case study The Upper Hunter Mining Dialogue for how these different types of social capital were developed in a real project.

FIGURE 4. Potential stakeholder network patterns.

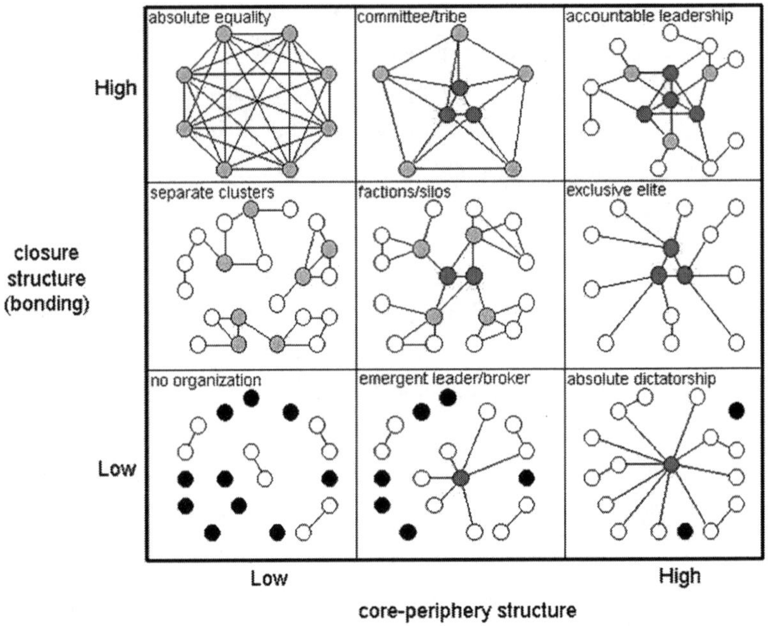

SOURCE: Boutilier, Robert. 2011. *A Stakeholder Approach to Issues Management* (New York: Business Expert Press). Reproduced with permission.

The vertical axis in Figure 4 shows the level of bonding between stakeholders; that is, the extent of strong relationships that enable adherence to social norms. A high level of bonding is like a village where everyone knows everyone else's business. If the stakeholder network is against you, changing your level of social licence will be very hard work. Attitudes in such groups change only slowly through exposure to external influences.

The horizontal axis shows links between the core or central organisation in a stakeholder network, and the periphery, those groups with few links to others. If there are few links between stakeholders, there is no organisation and it is difficult to earn a social licence. You would have to negotiate with each group separately and without any generally accepted norms between the groups; it would be slow and potentially fruitless work.

The stakeholder network patterns towards the top right of Figure 4 are more capable of issuing a valid and durable social licence and the stakeholder network patterns towards the lower left are less capable of issuing a valid and durable social licence. Ideally, stakeholder networks need a balance of strong and weak relationships between different organisations, like the pattern in the top right. The strong relationships enable the development of shared values and social norms and can build community cohesiveness. The weaker relationships enable different types of stakeholders to benefit from co-ordination. It's called the accountable leadership pattern because the periphery and semi-periphery are organised enough to hold the core accountable, but the core is strong enough to set and enforce rules and norms that everyone agrees with.

Let's look at a real stakeholder network.

Figure 5 shows the network of stakeholders who were approached to get involved in the Upper Hunter Mining Dialogue, a project to address the cumulative impacts of coal mining. The network map was developed from stakeholder interviews undertaken by my company in late 2010. We asked each stakeholder about the quality of their relationship with each other stakeholder and mapped the network using social network analysis software.[14] The map shows only the strongest relationships

....

FIGURE 5. Stakeholder network map for the Upper Hunter Mining Dialogue, April 2011.[13]

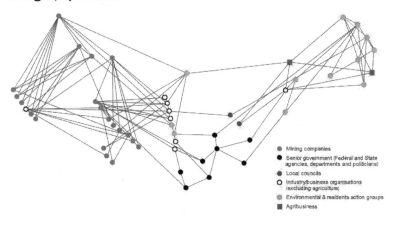

- ● Mining companies
- ● Senior government (Federal and State agencies, departments and politicians)
- ● Local councils
- ○ Industry/business organisations (excluding agriculture)
- ● Environmental & residents action groups
- ■ Agribusiness

....

between stakeholders. For a discussion of the case, see Chapter 5: Developing a Social Licence Strategy. Different patterns can be observed within this network.

For example, the top right hand corner looks like the 'perfect equality' pattern. These groups have access to the same information as one another and are likely to see things the same way. Most of them are environmental and residents' action groups, who, as shown in Chapter 5, granted the coal mining industry a 'low acceptance' level of social licence. The high level of bonding social capital between the environmental and residents' action groups suggested it would be hard to get them to change their view of mining without a) real action by the mining companies to address and b) helping them to form stronger relationships with others that might introduce new thinking into the groups.

On the left side the pattern looks more like the 'exclusive elite', with a handful of stakeholders – the four grey circles in the top left – maintaining relationships with many others who do not share relations with one another. These were the mining companies. Most of the relationships are between pairs of stakeholders, suggesting plenty of head office–site relationships, but not many strong relationships between sites, where local coordination would need to occur to address cumulative impacts. This pattern suggested to us that there was insufficient bonding capital between the mining companies to enable co-ordinated action on cumulative impacts.

In the middle of the network map, towards the bottom, we can see a cluster of dark green dots representing Federal and State government departments and agencies that have regulatory roles over the area. There are nine such stakeholders. If you count the number of relationships that each has with other government stakeholders you can see that one has five connections, and all the others have only one or two. This looks like the 'perfect dictatorship' pattern, except that the one with the most connections was not a dictator but simply had the widest range of strong relationships with others. This map shows that most of the government stakeholders were acting independently of one another with few strong ties to the community.

The stakeholder network map literally shows two sides of the community, with environmental and residents' action groups on one side, and mining companies on the other. The group in the centre, that one might hope could act as a bridge between the two sides, was government. But government appeared from our network map to be in a weak position to act in a co-ordinated way at that time.

To rebuild the social licence of the coal mining industry in this community, it needed to move to a stakeholder network pattern more like the 'accountable leadership' pattern on the top right of Figure 4. Stronger bonding social capital among the mining companies was required, and they needed to develop bridging capital between themselves and other parts of the stakeholder network. We needed some stakeholder engagement. To read more about the Upper Hunter Mining Dialogue, see the case study in Chapter 5: Developing a Social Licence Strategy.

Stakeholder engagement capabilities

Stakeholder engagement is the set of practices an organisation uses to involve stakeholders in decisions that affect them. It underpins your organisation's social licence, as it is the stakeholders who collectively issue the licence.

I believe every organisation can develop the capability for effective stakeholder engagement. Capabilities are recognised by management scholars as a source of performance and competitive advantage.[15] They are socially complex bundles of knowledge, skills and processes that are formed over time through interactions between different groups within an organisation. Capabilities have both cognitive and behavioural components; that is, they are partly about how we think, and partly about how we act.

A stakeholder engagement capability is present when an organisation a) identifies itself as closely linked with its stakeholders, and b) takes stakeholder needs into consideration in operational decisions. For managers to identify with stakeholders, they need to know and understand their stakeholders and recognise the interdependence between their organisation's interests and their stakeholder interests. This mind-set is part of a culture that enables managers to behave in socially responsible ways, by building co-operative, mutually reinforcing relationships.

Are you capable of earning a social licence?

To be really capable – as an organisation – to build your social licence you need four specific capabilities.

Ask a group of colleagues to rate the extent to which they agree or disagree with these statements. High levels of agreement with these statements suggest stronger capabilities.

STAKEHOLDER ENGAGEMENT

People in our organisation understand the linkages and inter-dependencies between us and our stakeholders that contribute to long-term prosperity.

Our managers routinely take into account stakeholder needs in business decisions.

STAKEHOLDER DIALOGUE

We respect our partners in dialogue by displaying empathy, honesty and non-manipulative intent.

INTEGRATING STAKEHOLDER VALUES

Our managers are able to effectively detect and transmit value-pertinent information about our stakeholders to all parts of the organisation to assist in business decision-making.

ACCOUNTABILITY

Our people believe that our organisation is accountable to stakeholders for our organisation's social, environmental and economic impacts.

Our business strategies, performance management and reporting processes effectively contribute to improved social, environmental and economic impacts.

CHAPTER 4

Measuring the Social Licence

THE SOCIAL LICENCE IS INTANGIBLE. It's a perception or evaluation of your company's legitimacy. You can't weigh it on a set of scales and you can't measure it with a ruler. But you *can* measure it.

To measure intangibles, we need to turn to the social sciences, where methods for the measurement of perceptions, values, beliefs and attitudes are well-developed. These things are measured in surveys, by asking people directly about their perceptions of the thing we want to know about.

Measuring perceptions

To measure perceptions, we should avoid asking over-simplified questions such as do you agree or disagree that this company has a social licence? For one, the social licence has levels. A simple statement of agreement or disagreement cannot tell you how high or low it is. And second, people might have different ideas in their minds about what the social licence is, or perhaps it's not even a term they are familiar with. Two different people who say 'yes' to a direct question about a company's social licence may have two entirely different things in mind. In that case the answers cannot be measuring the same thing, and we cannot rely on the results.

We need valid and reliable measures, so that we can be sure we are really measuring the thing we want to measure. Measures become reliable through large-scale testing and refinement in repeated surveys, work that has been underway at ACCSR and among our international colleagues for several years.

Stakeholder surveys

Our work has identified two potential ways of measuring the social licence through stakeholder surveys. One is by asking stakeholders whether they approve of or accept a particular company or operation. That gives us insight into the levels of social licence. We can compare the levels granted by different stakeholder groups as a basis for developing a social licence strategy.

The other way is to ask stakeholders about their perceptions of the four components of the social licence; whether they receive legitimate benefits from a company's presence; the state of social capital in relations between stakeholders and the company; the extent and nature of the company's contribution to the social contract, and the extent to which the company has become a trusted institution in the community. At the same time, we ask stakeholders to discuss their relationship with the company. This gives the necessary context for interpreting the social licence results and developing strategy.

Asking about the four components of the social licence provides more nuanced insights into the opportunities for strengthening the social licence, than asking solely about levels. For example, if we know that a company has strong relationships with stakeholders (social capital) but is assessed by stakeholders as weaker in providing legitimate benefits we would suggest adding new elements to the local community investment programs. If a company is strong in providing legitimate benefits but weak in its contribution to the social contract we would suggest extending community investment initiatives by involving a wider array of stakeholders or participating in regional initiatives.

Multi-item measures

Because each of the components of social licence captures several different aspects of stakeholder's perceptions of a company, we use multi-item measures, with each measure tapping a different aspect. Currently, we are using 14 statements to measure the social licence (see box below). We have also used a sub-set of these measures within a social impact assessment study where stakeholders were reflecting on a proposed development, rather than an existing one.

These statements form a neat fit against the four components of the social licence in studies undertaken so far by our colleagues in South America. But studies in Australia and Africa to date do not show clean differences between the four factors. The Australian and African work shows instead a single factor for the social licence. It is likely that the social licence is conceptualised differently in different cultural contexts and that measures of the social licence need local adaptations. We're working on it.

Important work is also being done on the social licence model and measures at Australia's national science agency, the CSIRO. It is clear that as our understanding of the social licence to operate develops, our measures will also evolve in the years to come.

The social licence questionnaire

You can include these questions in a social licence evaluation (see Conduct a Social Licence Evaluation in Chapter 5: Developing a Social Licence Strategy). Ask your stakeholders to answer these questions by stating the extent to which they agree or disagree with these statements on a scale of 1 to 5, where 1 represents strong disagreement and 5 represents strong agreement.

- We can gain from a relationship with [name of company].

- We need to have the cooperation of [name of company] to reach our most important goals.

- We are very satisfied with our relations with [name of company].

- [Name of company] does what is says it will do in its relations with our organisation.

- The presence of [name of company] is a benefit to us.

- [Name of company] listens to us.

- In the long term [name of company] makes a contribution to the well-being of the entire region.

- [Name of company] treats everyone fairly.

- [Name of company] respects our way of doing things.

- Our organisation and [name of company] have a similar vision for the future of this region.

- [Name of company] gives more support to those who it negatively affects.

- [Name of company] shares decision-making with us.

- [Name of company] takes account of our interests.

- [Name of company] openly shares information that is relevant to us.

To calculate a social licence score, calculate the mean of each stakeholder's responses to the group of questions. If you have many stakeholders you could group them into categories that make sense, for example, local government, environmental action groups, and so on. You can then calculate a stakeholder category score by finding the mean of all respondents' social licence scores in that category. Be sure to examine the standard deviation in the scores within the categories. Wide variation suggests an 'average' score might be hiding some important differences between stakeholders that would be useful to know about for developing strategies. You may need to find different criteria for creating groups so that the differences *between* the groups are bigger than the differences *within* the groups.

I am often asked, is our social licence score good or bad? And, how does our social licence compare to others? Establishing norms requires analysis of large datasets with, ideally, hundreds of thousands of stakeholder responses. So far, we have used the social licence measures with around 5000 stakeholders in 60 projects, so it is too early to establish guidance on norms.[16] You could use the indicative scoring ranges shown in Figure 6. We have divided the acceptance level into high, moderate and low based on our experience which suggests most stakeholders will rate organisations in the acceptance and approval levels most of the time.

FIGURE 6. Range of scores for different levels of social licence.

Full trust (dark green)	**4.5 to 4.99**
Approval (mid green)	**4.0 to 4.49**
High acceptance (light green)	**3.5 to 3.99**
Moderate acceptance (yellow)	**2.5 to 3.49**
Low acceptance (orange)	**2.5 to 3.00**
Withdrawn (red)	**1.0 to 2.49**

When to measure and how to chart results

Perceptions take time to change. Stakeholder perceptions of your social licence will change over time in response to your company's activities directly with stakeholders and in response to important social, environmental and economic issues in your region.

Unless there are dramatic events which could cause a sudden change in your social licence (like an acquisition or merger, announcement of a new development, closure of a site, etc.), annual measurement is usually enough. Measurement can be undertaken as a separate exercise, but

FIGURE 7. Sample graph of social licence scores granted by stakeholders.

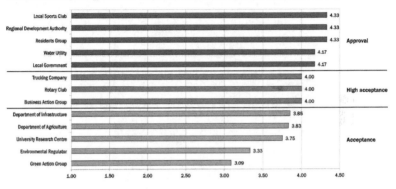

Social license to operate granted to a company by its stakeholders (Sample chart, scores out of 5)

Stakeholder	Score	Category
Local Sports Club	4.33	
Regional Development Authority	4.33	
Residents Group	4.33	Approval
Water Utility	4.17	
Local Government	4.17	
Trucking Company	4.00	
Rotary Club	4.00	High acceptance
Business Action Group	4.00	
Department of Infrastructure	3.85	
Department of Agriculture	3.83	
University Research Centre	3.75	Acceptance
Environmental Regulator	3.33	
Green Action Group	3.09	

more commonly it is combined within a stakeholder perception survey or social impact assessment. You can also combine the social licence measures with assessments of reputation, program evaluations and almost any other type of survey research that you might be planning with your stakeholders.

Depending on how many questions you want to ask, allow at least 15 minutes for the social licence assessment. The ratings style questions (see The social licence questionnaire above) will take about five minutes, and the remainder of the time should be used for open-ended questions that help you understand the context for the stakeholders' responses.

You can chart your results in Excel using an ordinary bar graph, showing the mean score across the social licence measures by individual stakeholder organisation (as in Figure 7), or by stakeholder category if you have a lot of stakeholders and need to summarise. If you are presenting results by stakeholder category, check to see if it makes sense to show mean scores. If you have a wide range of scores from different stakeholders within the same category, reporting only the mean could distort important information. In this case, it would be better to show all the stakeholder scores.

Combining social licence and stakeholder network insights

Insights into your company's social licence to operate can be dramatically enhanced when you overlay the results onto your stakeholder network map (see Chapter 3: Stakeholder Networks and Stakeholder Engagement Capabilities).

In the stakeholder network map of a hypothetical company shown in Figure 8, I have colour-coded the stakeholders by their level of social licence. Remember that the circles represent stakeholder organisations and the lines connecting them represent strong, social capital-filled relationships, relationships that are strong enough to enable the collaboration they desire.

We can see from Figure 8 that the stakeholder with the most connections to other stakeholders (which makes it the most influential stakeholder in the network), has actually withdrawn the social licence from the hypothetical company whose social licence is represented here. That stakeholder is represented by the big red circle on the upper left of the map. That's a problem for this company.

But an almost equally influential stakeholder is shown by the yellow circle

....

FIGURE 8. Levels of social licence within a stakeholder network.

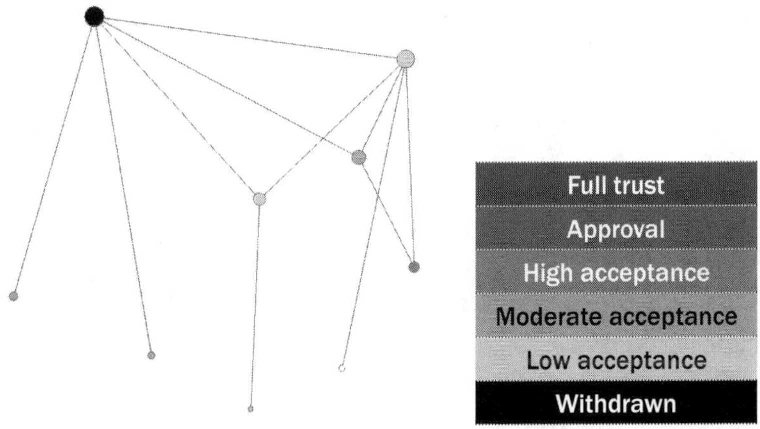

....

on the top right of the map. The yellow signifies that this stakeholder awards an acceptance level of the social licence. It is connected to other stakeholders who award the highest level of social licence (green) and another who grants a low acceptance level (orange). There's another stakeholder in the middle of the map who is also yellow. This group of stakeholders are moderately well connected with one another.

By combining information on the levels of social licence and the network structure of this community, we can make some useful suggestions for our hypothetical company. First, the company needs to understand which issues are causing the high and low levels of social licence (see next chapter). The company can then use its relatively strong position with the group of stakeholders on the right of the map to develop a shared response to the issues of concern that has more appeal to the red stakeholder. The good relationships enjoyed by the cluster on the right with the red stakeholder will help smooth a path towards direct engagement with the company.

When we think about the issues, the level of social licence and the network of relationships among the stakeholders we have the ingredients for developing a strategy to lift a company's social licence.

Case study: Measuring the social licence to operate at Xstrata Coal Queensland (now Glencore)[17]

Like many organisations, Xstrata Coal in Queensland regularly tests stakeholder perceptions and updates its community relations strategies. The company took the opportunity to assess its social licence to operate as part of its stakeholder perception survey in 2011. The mining company wanted to understand the level of social licence granted to it by its stakeholders at eight sites, as well as their perceptions of its environmental, social and economic performance. The mining company also wanted to understand how stakeholder organisations were related to each other, to highlight opportunities for collaborating with those organisations.

We interviewed nearly 800 stakeholders, representing organisations from a variety of sectors, including government, business, education and the environment. We also spoke to landholders and members of the community around the mines to understand their perspectives.

Issues maps were developed to show which issues were important to stakeholders and how those issues were linked together. The stakeholder network enabled mine managers to easily see areas where collaboration would be possible on these issues. Social licence scores allowed management to see which stakeholders gave higher or lower scores, and which issues underpinned the ratings.

The sites used this information to update their community engagement plans with the aim of improving their social licence with key environmental, community and government stakeholders.

CHAPTER 5

Developing a
Social Licence Strategy

A SOCIAL LICENCE STRATEGY is essentially a stakeholder engagement strategy for organisations to navigate complex socio-political environments. Basic stakeholder engagement strategies would consider stakeholders on a group by group basis and may be good enough if there is little complexity in your operations, value chain or socio-political environment. A social licence strategy is better suited if you are dealing with complexity because it incorporates the interactions between multiple stakeholders and issues.

In this chapter I will describe the basic steps in developing a social licence strategy: identify your stakeholders; understand their issues; measure the level of social licence in the stakeholder network; and choose tactics to strengthen your social licence based on your diagnosis.

How to identify stakeholders

Stakeholders become stakeholders because they have an issue with or interest in your organisation. They might be affected by your operations or want to influence your operations in some way. Stakeholders get organised around issues.

Therefore, a useful way to identify stakeholders is to start with a list of issues relevant to your organisation. There are many good methods for developing a list of relevant issues. You could examine the list of 'aspects' in the Global Reporting Initiative to identify the relevant ones for your organisation. You could look at sustainability reports of other companies in your industry or sector to see what issues they cover. You could analyse media coverage of your organisation, or analyse complaints about your organisation. You should also list the people and groups your organisation already deals with on a day-to-day basis.

But you knew that already, right? So here's the thing that will lift the quality of your stakeholder identification methods to help ensure comprehensive identification.

Ask the question, *who else has a stake in an issue that your stakeholders care about?*

That one simple question can lead you to discover stakeholders who may be only at the margins of your considerations, or not yet on your radar at all.

Try asking your stakeholders directly, 'Who else has an interest in the issues that are important to you?' You could find yourself embarking on a rich and fascinating dialogue that will lead to better opportunities for engagement and issues management, and strengthen the foundation for your social licence.

Once you have developed your stakeholder list, you will need to talk directly to them to obtain information on the issues that are important to them and the level of social licence they grant. You can do this yourself as part of a structured engagement through individual or group meetings, or online surveys. Or you can engage an independent social researcher to help you with this step (see Chapter 4: Measuring the Social Licence).

An important point to remember is that stakeholders are self-defining. They define themselves in relation to the impacts and benefits of a company and not in relation to a physical distance. If they believe they have a stake in your organisation, you can't avoid dealing with them on the basis they are not legitimate stakeholders or they don't have a legitimate issue. That would be like driving a car while wearing a blindfold.

Steps for stakeholder identification:
- Identify the issues relevant to your organisation.
- Work out which stakeholders care about these issues.
- Ask your stakeholders, who else cares about the issues that are important to you?

Opinion leaders and followers

For purposes of social licence strategy, your stakeholder identification should focus on *opinion leaders*. The opinion leaders are those stakeholders who lead organisations or groups with whom your organisation must interact to fully understand its impacts or develop and implement its strategies.

They are opinion leaders by virtue of their ability to make decisions, take actions or represent other stakeholders. They have some degree of power through their organisations. They can influence perceptions by their behaviour and their relationships with other stakeholders. That makes them influential. Your social licence strategy and the research you conduct to develop your social licence strategy must focus on these stakeholders.

They might be leaders of community or environmental groups, heads of government departments or agencies, leaders of industry associations, or have some other official or unofficial representative role in the community.

The *opinion followers* are in comparison the passive majority. They will not act in a co-ordinated way unless they have a problem they believe your organisation can address and they can get organised to do something about it. They can become organised by forming new groups or joining existing groups. They are the general public.

Your social licence strategy should provide opportunities for more passive stakeholders to become involved in, hear about or read about your organisation's activities. You can track their opinions and perceptions through traditional market research methods.

Understand the issues

There are many different ways of identifying and analysing issues. You could examine media coverage about your company, look at scientific research or government reports related to your industry, or scan discussion groups on the internet. All of these are helpful.

But because the social licence is issued by your stakeholders, the best source to go to understand the issues is the stakeholders themselves. Talk to them. A semi-structured interview guide is very useful for these conversations, as it will enable consistency and comparability of the questions, while leaving opportunities for probing the topics that stakeholders raise. It is very important that these discussions be impartial and unbiased. The questions I like to use are:[18]

- Tell me about your organisation's relationship with [company X]?

- (Probe for examples that can elaborate or clarify if needed)

- Why is that important to you?

- What other issues are connected to that?

Take detailed notes, verbatim if you can. This is the information you will need to map the issues. Social network analysis software can be used to map issues as shown in Figure 9. The issues shown in Figure 9 were mentioned by stakeholders of a major road-widening project I worked on a few years ago. Two issues came up repeatedly in stakeholder interviews undertaken before works commenced: noise and traffic management during construction. We expected to hear about those.

FIGURE 9. Sample issues network.

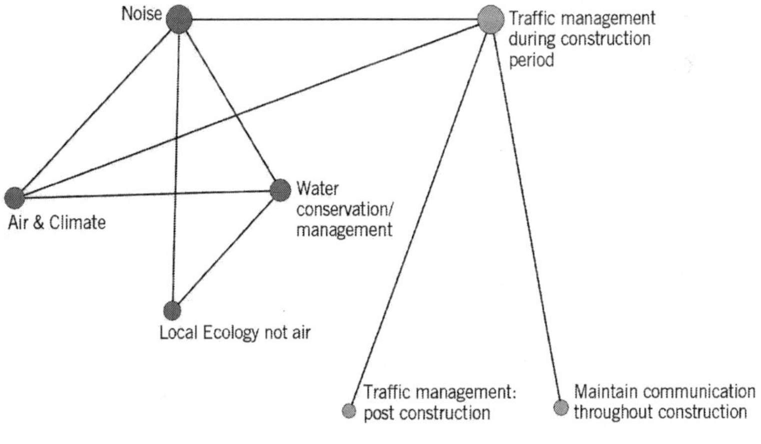

What was more interesting was that a range of environmental concerns sat beneath the issue of noise. The issues analysis showed that if stakeholders were to complain about noise, they would be likely to raise other complaints related to impacts on the local environment, not just them personally. Very localised biodiversity and water management plans, supported by appropriate communications, would be needed for this project, if the construction company's social licence were to be preserved.

If you don't have social network analysis software, you can use the same free-hand network mapping technique I described in Chapter 3: Stakeholder Networks and Stakeholder Engagement Capabilities, using the names of issues to label the circles, instead of the names of stakeholders.

Conduct a social licence evaluation

Your social licence evaluation focuses on understanding the level of social licence granted to you by each of your stakeholders and how they are connected to one another. In Chapters 3 and 4 I have outlined steps for mapping your stakeholder network and measuring your social licence. The issues analysis, network mapping and social licence scores are the elements of the social licence evaluation. You can combine these elements in a single interview with each of your opinion-leader stakeholders as described above. I like to allow up to an hour for these in-depth interviews.

Steps for conducting a social licence evaluation

- Identify your key stakeholders

    - These should be organisations with which your company has a relationship.

    - Include stakeholders that are critical of you, not just those you like.

    - Ask yourself what issues your stakeholders care about, and then ask yourself, who else has an interest in these issues? This will help you identify additional stakeholders who might be important to include.

- Plan your social licence evaluation

    - Consider what information you need from this evaluation and how you intend to use the results.

    - Consider the use of qualified independent researchers to ensure an unbiased approach (see box about social desirability).

- Decide on your method

    - Will you undertake telephone interviews or face-to-face interviews? These methods are generally better than self-complete surveys as they allow for discussion and help you understand the context for stakeholders' responses.

- Draft the social licence survey

    - Using a combination of open-ended and ratings style questions will give you the best results.

- Include other questions that will help you contextualise your results, like assessments of your social, environmental or economic performance.

- Invite the stakeholders to participate

- Conduct the research and analyse the results

- Use the results to develop your social licence strategy (see Chapter 5: Developing a Social Licence Strategy)

Avoiding social desirability bias

Social desirability bias is a well-recognised phenomenon in social sciences research,[19] including stakeholder perception surveys that are used to measure the social licence to operate.

It means that research participants will give you the answer they think you want, instead of what they really think. They might do this for a range of reasons, such as wanting to please you, being polite, or being fearful that if they give the 'wrong' answer they might lose funding or other benefits that your company provides.

To overcome this tendency, use independent experts in social sciences research. Stakeholders are often more comfortable saying what they really think to an independent third party. The independent third party should be a qualified expert in research and follow ethical research practices.

Choose tactics to build your social licence

After you have conducted your social licence evaluation and analysed the results, you are ready to develop your strategy.

If your social licence is fairly low, your strategy will focus on providing legitimate benefits for your stakeholders and building social capital in stakeholder relationships.

If your social licence is in the acceptance or approval range, you already have a moderately effective strategy for providing legitimate benefits and you need to work on both the social capital and social contract components of the social licence.

Some examples of good tactics for building your social licence are shown in Table 2. You should choose tactics that will help you respond to the issues that are most important to your stakeholders. The suggestions in Table 2 are not an absolute categorisation; tactics can work well for different types of social licence strategies. You can also look at Table 3 in Chapter 6: Using International Frameworks for Your Social Licence, which draws on the International Guidance Standard for Social Responsibility, ISO 26000, to suggest tactics for each component of your social licence to operate.

TABLE 2. Tactics for building your social licence

	Ensuring legitimate benefits for communities	Building social capital in stakeholder relations	Building the social contract
Tactics	• Donations • Investments in local infrastructure, e.g. roads, bridges, schools, hospitals • Volunteering • Local purchasing • Sponsorship of community events • Gathering input through surveys and consultation	• Dialogue • Community advisory groups • Open house events • Partnerships that respond to specific issues	• Multi-stakeholder partnerships to address social, environmental or economic challenges • Participation in regional development projects • Community leadership in decision-making • Community capacity building through training • Establish grievance mechanisms
Form of control	• Company	• Company	• Shared between company and stakeholders
Risks and challenges	• Dependency on company handouts	• Selective engagement may alienate parts of community	• Resource intensive • Progress may be slower and more difficult

Achieving the highest level of social licence, institutionalised trust, must be based on solid achievement of the other three factors. At this level, changes in stakeholder or company personnel do not disrupt the social contract. Grievance procedures operate smoothly and effectively. You are working effectively within multi-stakeholder initiatives that support the long-term prosperity of the region where you operate. You are regarded as approachable and accountable for your organisation's impacts. The community identifies with your industry or organisation.

Starbucks in Seattle, Universal Studios in Los Angeles and Airbus in Toulouse are examples of companies that are strongly identified with local communities and are likely to enjoy a very high social licence with local stakeholders.

A special word on grievance mechanisms

Creation of a social contract at a local level involves negotiating fairness and justice with stakeholders. A complaints or grievances resolution process is a necessary element. This should be culturally appropriate. For example, at the Lihir gold mine in Papua New Guinea, the customary dispute handling instrument is a *gorgor*, made from the leaves of a ginger plant. When a *gorgor* is placed on the mine site, traditional owners are signalling that talks are needed. Work stops until the matter is resolved.[20]

The goal of a complaints management system is to provide an alternative to legal procedures through collaboration between parties to resolve issues in a more efficient and collaborative way, which builds community ownership of solutions.

The complaints mechanism must offer the community a clear, formal process that is publicly available, accessible, widely understood and provides an agreed channel for complaints. Best practice complaints mechanisms are predictable: they offer clear processes and timeframes for redress of concerns. They are also transparent in the carrying out of agreed procedures. The complaints mechanism is ideally co-created with community members, for example with a community reference group.

An effective complaints mechanism requires sound definitions and boundaries about the type and degree of complaints that will be addressed through the mechanism. This may include, but not be limited to, community concerns or grievances about the performance or behaviour of a company, its contractors or employees. Criteria should then be set to indicate how different levels of complaints will be dealt with. On one hand, complaints classed as 'minor', according to the agreed definition, may require a phone call or site visit. On the other hand, complaints classed as 'major' may require remediation works, mediation or even legal attention.

Advice from the community reference group and information from baseline studies, one-on-one consultations, open houses, telephone hotlines or websites can help to review continually the types and degree of issues which may be best addressed through the complaints mechanism.

At a bare minimum, the complaints mechanism should act as a formal 'clearing house' for recording all complaints related to your operations. Records of every complaint channelled through the mechanism should be kept, with notes about who lodged the complaint, when, any actions taken, and, where possible, the solutions agreed and implemented.

All complaints recorded, actions taken and outcomes achieved should be reviewed at regular intervals to evaluate success and to refine the complaints mechanism as needed.

Case studies on social licence strategy

BMA's Local Buying Program[21]

The BHP Billiton Mitsubishi Alliance (BMA) operates seven coal mines in central Queensland in Australia, accounting for more than a quarter of Australia's annual coal exports and 28% of the world's seaborne trade in metallurgical coal. It employs about 6000 people and produces 50 million tonnes of coal annually. The closest towns to its mines are Moranbah (population 8965), Dysart (population 3003), Blackwater (population 4837) and Emerald (population 12,895).[22]

The company has a longstanding community partnerships program that has entailed extensive funding for education, community infrastructure and indigenous programs over the years. At one point community investment totalled A$23 million per annum.[23]

It has had its share of controversy. For example, BMA has experienced conflict with trade unions[24] and others about employment of locals, conditions of employment and the use of fly-in, fly-out workers.

In mid-2012 it launched a local buying program aimed at building the capacity small businesses supply goods and services to the company. The program targets businesses with fewer than 25 employees in the four towns near its mines. The program operates through a partnership between BMA and the Mackay-Isaac-Whitsunday Regional Economic Development Corporation (REDC), a non-profit, membership-based peak economic development organisation with local government support. REDC established a subsidiary called Community Resourcing (C-Res)[25] to administer the program.

For every contract that is let by BMA through C-Res, a percentage is allocated to a Local Buying Community Foundation that provides grants for local business training and development and broader economic and community development. The program includes education and training programs for small business and employs Community Development Officers to act as mentors to registered suppliers.

By the end of March 2013 there were 287 approved suppliers registered in the program, with 397 contracts awarded to 111 suppliers and a total spend of A$6.44 million for the year to date.[26]

This local procurement program is an excellent example of providing legitimate benefits to communities and should provide a solid foundation for BMA's social licence. It spreads economic benefits to a sector that is often left out of the supply chain of large companies because it is easier for big companies to deal with fewer large suppliers than many small suppliers. The partnership with REDC with its deep local roots and the use of an independent body managed through REDC contributes to legitimacy.

Its local capacity-building features push it towards the 'social contract' component of the social licence model. To strengthen the Local Buying Program's contribution to the social contract it could consider broadening the number of large companies making contracts available to the local community. Other members of the REDC would seem to be the obvious choice in the first instance.

The Upper Hunter Mining Dialogue[27]

Coal mining in the Upper Hunter valley in New South Wales has been part of the social and economic fabric of the community since European settlement. But since the mid-1990s, coal mining expanded rapidly, and with that came increasing cumulative impacts on air quality, water, traffic, housing prices and a host of other environmental, social and economic stresses. Residents' action and environmental groups emerged to campaign against growth of the coal industry. While some mining was good, too much mining was not.

In 2010 community opposition played a role in the successful campaign to stop the Bickham Coal Mine being approved. Then there was an exposé of dust problems on the Australian Broadcasting Corporation's influential current affairs program, *Four Corners*.[28]

The coal miners needed to rebuild their social licence. Although they collectively employed around 12,000 people in a regional population of less than 40,000, community acceptance was at rock-bottom.

The NSW Minerals Council, the industry association for miners in NSW, embarked on a program to rebuild the industry's social licence. They engaged my company[29] to conduct a baseline study that included measurement of the social licence. The social licence of the industry was rated at the acceptance level by most of the 93 stakeholders surveyed. Environmental and residents action groups on average rated it at a 'low acceptance' level. No stakeholders rated it at the 'approval' level.

The NSWMC embarked on a community outreach program in early 2011. It started with individual meetings between industry representatives and as many of the stakeholders as possible to discuss the results and ask for cooperation. We also organised community information evenings in three towns in the area. Invitations to the public were published in local newspapers. A series of posters was created to describe the research results. We took the opportunity to invite public feedback on the issues of importance, by placing coloured sticky dots next to the issues they thought were most important. Mining company personnel were on hand to discuss the results and any other topic a person may care to raise.

The outreach program was quickly followed by a stakeholder workshop to which all 93 of the original research participants were invited, plus a few more who said they were interested. This workshop aimed to get a clear mandate from stakeholders about the priorities for action and invite them to get involved. The result was that four working groups were formed related to land management, social impacts, water and health and air quality.

Working together on this project enabled the mining companies to develop stronger bonding social capital. No-one wanted to let the group down and they spurred each other on. The outreach program with community stakeholders helped to form bridging social capital and the necessary co-ordination between stakeholders to get cumulative impacts management programs off the ground.

Two years later, a number of programs had been agreed and were underway; for example, a grazing trial to measure the productivity of land that has been mined and restored to pasture; and a program to develop industry management practices for emissions using predictive forecasting.

The Upper Hunter Mining Dialogue began as an initiative that targeted the social contract component of the social licence model. But it soon became apparent that to succeed, the mining company would need to build social capital and bring more legitimate benefits to the region.

The public conflict of 2010 seems to have reduced. Time will tell if the Upper Hunter Mining Dialogue will succeed in restoring the coal industry's social licence to operate.

Social licence strategy: Four tips for success

1. Bond before you bridge

   - Establishing trust and shared values within your own group or company must occur before you try to build trust and shared values with other groups. This is important so that your organisation can act consistently in its relations with communities and other stakeholders.

   - Working together with stakeholders on programs that enable you to learn about one another and flexibly address community needs is more durable than implementing a pre-conceived stakeholder program.

   - Bridging with external stakeholders should proceed from easy to difficult stakeholders.

2. Promote equitable relations among internal and external stakeholders

   - Promote meritocracy among internal stakeholders by quantifying and documenting skills and knowledge.

   - Break down internal silos or work across them.

   - Reject extortion, bribery and nepotism.

   - Appeal to expanded identities to reduce factionalism: family => community => region => nation.

---

3. Be explicit and manage expectations

   – Consistent and transparent processes for dealing with stakeholders will work better than a fixed policy.

   – Publicise your processes, policies and the reasons for your decisions.

4. Get involved with shared problems

• Take the initiative on shared problems with all sectors of the community.

• See how your organisation can get involved in solving problems related to economic development, training and education, health and safety, public infrastructure, or security and public safety.

• Involvement creates opportunities to shape the structure of the stakeholder network.

Adapted from materials developed by Dr Robert Boutilier for ACCSR's public master class: How to Earn and Maintain a Social Licence to Operate, 23 November 2013.

CHAPTER 6

Using International Frameworks for Your Social Licence

THOUSANDS OF ORGANISATIONS use voluntary international frameworks for planning or reporting on their social responsibilities and impacts. Many of these frameworks provide useful background and context for the social licence to operate, such as the UN Global Compact with its ten principles to guide organisational behaviour, the OECD Guidelines for Multinationals and the United Nations Principles for Business and Human Rights.

In this chapter I describe the major frameworks that can be applied as part of a social licence evaluation, strategy or for public reporting: ISO 26000 Guidance Standard for Social Responsibility; AA1000 Stakeholder Engagement Standard; Integrated Reporting (<IR>); the UN Guiding Principles for Business and Human Rights and the Global Reporting Initiative G4 framework.

A brief guide to using international frameworks for social responsibility together with the social licence

TABLE 3. The role of selected voluntary frameworks in social licence tasks

SOCIAL LICENCE TASK	PROCESS	TOOL	SPECIFIC GUIDANCE
Social licence assessments	Identifying stake-holders	ISO 26000	Section 5.3.2
Social licence strategies	Engaging with stake-holders	ISO 26000	Section 2.21, 5.3.3, 6.3, 6.8, 7.6.1.
		AA1000SES	Guidance on principles and processes
		GRI	Reporting principle: stakeholder inclusiveness
		<IR>	Reporting principle: stakeholder responsiveness
		UN Guiding Principles on Business & Human Rights	The 'Protect, Respect and Remedy' framework provides foundational principles on which a social licence can be built. The 'Remedy' or grievance mechanisms are necessary to achievement of the social contract component of the SLO model.
Social licence reporting	Performance measurement and management	GRI	Standard disclosures on stakeholder engagement G4-24 to G4-27 and as relevant within disclosures on management approach. Indicators can suggest measures relevant to the issues or practices that underpin your social licence
		<IR>	Social and relationship capital

Social licence assessment and strategy

ISO 26000 Guidance Standard on Social Responsibility

The ISO 26000 Guidance Standard on Social Responsibility, published in 2010, provides a comprehensive definition and framework for social responsibility in any organisation. It provides both principles-based and practical guidance relevant to the social licence to operate. It can be used to help plan your social licence assessment and develop your social licence strategy.

PRINCIPLE: RESPECT FOR STAKEHOLDER INTERESTS. One of the principles of social responsibility is that an organisation 'should respect, consider and respond to the interests of its stakeholders' (ISO 26000:4.5, p. 12). This principle sets out the actions that an organisation should take, such as identifying its stakeholders, assessing their ability to engage with and influence the organisation, considering their views and taking into account the relation between their views and the broader expectations of society.

These actions can form part of a social licence evaluation, as described in Chapter 4: Measuring the Social Licence.

ISO 26000 also provides helpful guidance for stakeholder identification and engagement.

All of the 'core subjects' within ISO 26000 contain issues that may need attention within your social licence strategy. However, the subjects of human rights, and community involvement and development, provide especially useful guidance for social licence strategies.

CORE SUBJECT: HUMAN RIGHTS. It is impossible to earn, maintain or build a social licence in the absence of respect for and protection of human rights. ISO 26000 6.3 describes eight issues that should be addressed by organisations: due diligence; human rights risk situations; avoidance of complicity; resolving grievances; discrimination and vulnerable groups; civil and political rights; economic, social and cultural rights; and rights at work.

All of these issues need to be addressed to build the most basic block of the social licence: legitimacy of benefits. Any benefit that may flow from your organisation's activities or operations will not be experienced by stakeholders as a true benefit if any of these human rights issues are present and remain unaddressed. Positive actions in some of these areas can help build the social capital and social contract elements of your social licence. For example, risk situations like poverty, drought or complex value chains can be addressed through participation in multi-stakeholder initiatives.

PepsiCo in Ethiopia

PepsiCo, one of the largest food and beverage manufacturers in the world, has developed a program to tackle malnutrition and build economic resilience among farmers in Ethiopia, while improving security of an essential ingredient in many of its products: chickpeas.

Partnering with the World Food Program, the United States Agency for International Development, and a local NGO, the program aims to increase production through improved agricultural practices.

I don't know if PepsiCo conceived this as a social licence program. I imagine the company was probably thinking about resource security and bolstering the economic resilience of its supply chain. But it is a program that can help avert human rights risks by addressing causes of poverty and malnutrition. It should build PepsiCo's social contract directly in the region where it works with chickpea farmers and contribute in that way to its social licence to operate.

CORE SUBJECT: COMMUNITY INVOLVEMENT AND DEVELOPMENT. ISO 26000 6.8 section on community involvement and development provides direct guidance for establishing a social licence. It describes principles such as being part of the community, respecting the rights of communities to make their own decisions, respecting local ways of doing things and recognising the value of working in partnership. Following these principles is a recipe for success in building your social licence.

Section 6.8 also describes seven issues: community involvement; education and culture; employment creation and skills; technology development and access; wealth and income creation; health; and social investment. The related actions and expectations for each of these issues provide a rich array of possibilities for organisational actions to address the three foundation components of the social licence: legitimate benefits, social capital and the social contract. In this chapter I have suggested which component of the social licence is best exemplified by each of the related expectations and actions within Section 6.8 on community involvement and development.

For example, your social licence strategy should be founded on legitimate benefits to the community. Typically we think of providing jobs and perhaps some local purchasing. ISO 26000 suggests we could take a more nuanced approach to jobs and procurement, for example, by analysing the impact of investment decisions or technology on employment creation, or through capacity-building programs that get local suppliers into bigger value chains – either yours or other companies. ISO 26000 also encourages us to think about health, education and cultural benefits that should flow from our organisation's involvement in a community.

Building social capital requires dialogue, collaboration and accountability, which can be achieved through ISO 26000's recommended actions such as consulting local communities about how development that affects them will be carried out, maintaining transparent relationships with local government and local partnerships that make use of complementary resources.

In building the social contract element of your social licence, ISO 26000's recommended actions such as respect for local ways, entering local capacity-building programs related to technology or entrepreneurship and promoting economic diversification, are all helpful.

You may have different thoughts about which element of the social licence framework is best exemplified by each of the actions in Table 4. That's OK. The boundaries between the components of the framework are fuzzy and different ways of implementing each action could lead to different social licence outcomes.

ING_FRAMEWORK FOR COMPLEX TIMES

THE SOCIAL LICENCE TO OPERATE:
YOUR MANAGEMENT FRAMEWORK FOR COMPLEX TIMES

TABLE 4. Community development actions in ISO 26000 classified by social licence component.

ISSUE	RELATED ACTIONS AND EXPECTATIONS (SHORT FORM)	PRIMARY SLO COMPONENT
Community involvement	Consult representative community groups in determining priorities for social investment and community development	Social capital
	Consult and accommodate communities, including indigenous people, on the terms and conditions of development that affect them	Social capital
	Participate in local associations	Social contract
	Maintain transparent relationships with local government officials and political representatives	Social capital
	Encourage and support people to be volunteers for community service	Social capital
	Contribute to policy formulation and ... development programs	Social contract
Education and culture	Promote and support education at all levels	Legitimate benefits
	Promote learning opportunities for vulnerable or discriminated groups	Legitimate benefits
	Encourage the enrolment of children in formal education	Legitimate benefits
	Promote cultural activities ... recognise and value the local cultures and cultural traditions	Social contract
	Facilitate human rights education and awareness raising	Social capital
	Conserve and protect cultural heritage	Legitimate benefits
	Promote the use of traditional knowledge and technologies of indigenous	Social contract

ISSUE	RELATED ACTIONS AND EXPECTATIONS (SHORT FORM)	PRIMARY SLO COMPONENT
Employment creation and skills	Analyse the impact of investment decisions on employment creation	Legitimate benefits
	Consider the impact of technology choice on employment	Legitimate benefits
	Consider the impact of outsourcing decisions on employment creation	Legitimate benefits
	Consider the benefit of creating direct employment rather than using temporary work arrangements	Legitimate benefits
	Participate in local and national skills development programmes	Social contract
	Help develop or improve skills development programs in the community ... in partnership with others	Social contract
	Give special attention to vulnerable groups with regard to employment and capacity building	Legitimate benefits
	Promote conditions necessary to create employment	Social contract
Technology development and access	Help develop innovative technologies that can help solve social and environmental issues in local communities	Social contract
	Contribute to the development of low-cost technologies	Legitimate benefits
	Develop...local and traditional knowledge and technologies while protecting the community's right to that knowledge and technology	Social contract
	Engage in partnerships with organisations, such as universities ...	Social contract
	Adopt practices that allow technology transfer and diffusion	Social contract

ISSUE	RELATED ACTIONS AND EXPECTATIONS (SHORT FORM)	PRIMARY SLO COMPONENT
Wealth and income creation	Consider the economic and social impact of entering or leaving a community	Legitimate benefits
	Support appropriate initiatives to stimulate diversification of existing economic activity	Social contract
	Give preference to local suppliers of products and services	Legitimate benefits
	Strengthen the ability of and opportunities for locally based suppliers to contribute to value chains	Legitimate benefits
	Assist organisations to operate within the appropriate legal framework	Social contract
	Engage in economic activities with organisations to address poverty	Social contract
	Contribute to durable programs and partnerships that assist...women and ... vulnerable groups to establish businesses	Social contract
	Encourage the efficient use of available resources	Social contract
	Make procurement opportunities more easily accessible to community organisations	Legitimate benefits
	Support organisations and persons that bring needed products and services to the community	Social contract
	Help develop community-based associations of entrepreneurs	Social contract
	Fulfil tax responsibilities	Legitimate benefits
	Contribute to superannuation and pensions for employees	Legitimate benefits

ISSUE	RELATED ACTIONS AND EXPECTATIONS (SHORT FORM)	PRIMARY SLO COMPONENT
Health	Eliminate negative health impacts of ... the organisation's activities	Legitimate benefits
	Promote good health	Legitimate benefits
	Raise awareness about health threats and major diseases and their prevention	Social capital
	Supporting long lasting and universal access to essential health care services and to clean water	Social contract
Social investment	Promote community development in planning social investment projects	Social contract
	Avoid actions that perpetuate a community's dependence on the organisation's philanthropic activities	Legitimate benefits
	Assess community-related initiatives and report to the community ... to identify improvements	Social capital
	Partner with other organisations, including government, business or NGOs to ... maximise and make use of complementary resources ...	Social capital
	Contribute to programs that provide access to food and other essential products for vulnerable groups	Legitimate benefits

The United Nations Guiding Principles for Business and Human Rights

The UN Guiding Principles for Business and Human Rights were endorsed by the UN Human Rights Council on 16 June 2011. Developed by UN Special Representative John Ruggie over a six-year period with the support of business and civil society, the Principles translate UN Declarations, Covenants and treaties addressing human rights into an elegant, practical and powerful framework for business.

In his recent book, *Just Business*,[30] Ruggie describes a visit the Yanacocha mine in Peru in 2006 which 'did not enjoy a strong "social licence to operate – broad acceptance of the company's operation by the community"' (p. xxxix). What he saw there showed him what it would take to develop stronger protection against corporate-related human rights harms.

The 'Protect, Respect, and Remedy' Framework affirms the state duty to protect, the corporate responsibility to respect, and access to remedies or grievance mechanisms. The corporate responsibility to respect human rights comprises a policy commitment by business, a due diligence process for identifying, preventing, mitigating and accounting for impacts on human rights, and a process to enable remediation of any adverse human rights impacts a company might cause or contribute to.

A company that commits to and enacts the Principles in its relationships with local communities will be well on its way to earning a durable social licence to operate.

AA1000 Stakeholder Engagement Standard

The AA1000 Stakeholder Engagement Standard (2011) has been developed by the international think-tank and consulting company, AccountAbility. The Stakeholder Engagement Standard is a practical, basic how-to manual for planning and organising stakeholder engagement. It focuses on organisational processes for planning and can be applied within a social licence approach. However, used on its own it is unlikely to be powerful enough to guide organisations through the complexity in stakeholder networks, relationships and the socio-political environment that requires management through social licence strategies.

Reporting your social licence

Reporting to stakeholders about progress and challenges to your social licence is important for the same reasons as any public reporting on social responsibility and sustainable development. It demonstrates accountability for impacts, provides a basis for dialogue with stakeholders, and drives performance improvement.

The two major reporting frameworks, Integrated Reporting (<IR>), and the Global Reporting Initiative Framework, can be used together to guide public disclosure of your organisation's approach and impact. Neither framework offers advice on how to measure your social licence. You can use the measures in this book for that. However, <IR> provides direct, principles-based guidance on social capital and relationships, which are a foundation for the social licence to operate.

Experience in South Africa and elsewhere shows that those best prepared for the emergence of <IR> already have a good understanding of sustainability reporting. I recommend using both <IR> and the GRI. <IR> will help you focus on how you create and transform value for the company and its stakeholders through stakeholder relationships and your social licence. GRI will help you report at a more detailed level how you are handling the material issues that stakeholders evaluate when they grant your social licence at either a lower, or a higher level.

Integrated reporting

<IR> is rapidly emerging as the new high-water mark for corporate reporting. It asks reporters to answer the question, how do we create, transform or destroy value over the short, medium and long term? This

information is important for investors, by allowing them to make more informed decisions, but is also of great interest to a broad range of stakeholders.

The International Integrated Reporting Committee[31] which is overseeing the development of <IR> conceptualises organisations as a stock and flow of capitals, or resources. They are financial capital, manufactured capital, intellectual capital, social and relationship capital, human capital and natural capital.

It is only by building social and relationship capital that an organisation can develop and maintain its social licence to operate. Integrated reporting asks organisations to report on the interdependencies between the different forms of capital and how each contributes to creating value over time.

The social licence framework in this book is intended primarily as an operational and measurement framework. It can underpin reporting on social and relationship capital within the integrated reporting framework by enabling managers to understand the context within which they must develop their social licence, the conditions required to maintain it, and what makes their social licence rise or fall. A discussion of these factors should be incorporated into integrated reports.

The Global Reporting Initiative Guidelines

The Global Reporting Initiative is the world's gold standard for sustainability reporting. The latest version, G4, asks organisations to report on their most material 'aspects'. These are the subjects or topics that are most important to both your organisation and your stakeholders.

The G4's guidance for analysing aspects includes understanding the expectations of stakeholders about the appropriateness of your actions and your transparency about aspect. The GRI also asks you to prioritise stakeholders, which can be done through stakeholder network mapping as shown in Chapter 3: Stakeholder Networks and Stakeholder Engagement Capabilities.

The report itself can also be used as a tool for engagement and dialogue with local communities, contributing to building the social capital component of your social licence. Using a consistent and robust framework like G4 promotes accountability. This is important for building the social contract component of your social licence.

....

CHAPTER 7

Conclusion

THE SOCIAL LICENCE TO OPERATE began as a metaphor to bring attention to the need for companies to earn acceptance or approval from their host communities. Today, the social licence is emerging as a management framework for complex times. We are still at the beginning of our knowledge about the social licence. The continuing interplay between research and practice will yield better tools and more insights in the future. But for now, here's what I know. The social licence looks at stakeholder and community relations through a political lens. If a company is to engage effectively with its local communities and stakeholders it must negotiate and ensure a fair and equitable distribution of benefits and impacts from its presence, over the near and longer term.

The social licence is not a synonym for acts of philanthropy or community investment, which on their own do not guarantee a social licence. Negotiation of benefits and impacts entails acknowledging, respecting and collaborating with stakeholders on issues of mutual concern.

Stakeholders and communities are self-defining. They define themselves in relation to the impacts and benefits of a company and not in relation to a physical distance.

A company that wants to restore, earn, maintain or improve its social licence has to first understand the network structure of its communities.

CONCLUSION

Who are the stakeholders? What are their interests and needs? How do these cause divisions in communities and how, and on what issues, can stakeholders and companies work together? These fundamental questions need answers to be able to develop a meaningful social licence to operate.

Effective grievance mechanisms are essential for the effective operation of a social licence. Grievance mechanisms enable imbalances in benefits and impacts to be redressed as they occur. They help prevent the social licence from being eroded.

The social licence is dynamic. It changes as communities' needs and expectations change, and in response to company behaviour. Because it is dynamic, the social licence needs to be continuously monitored and when necessary adapted. The social licence takes into account the history of communities' internal dynamics and community–company relations. The more complexity encountered, the higher the need for empirical, detailed and careful measurement and negotiation of the social licence. What you don't know *can* hurt you.

The social licence to operate is measurable and can be easily incorporated into your regular stakeholder perception studies.

There is no substitute for direct stakeholder engagement in the measurement of the social licence.

The foundation of the social licence is trust. Trust is earned through consistent trustworthy behaviour every day over a long time.

....

Notes

1. Pritchard, M. and Claughton, D. 2010. Bickham Coal mine rejected. ABC Rural On-line Friday, 14 May. Available from: **http://www.abc.net.au/rural/content/2010/s2899704.htm** (accessed 21 March 2013).

2. For example, Joyce, S. and Thomson, I. 2000. Earning a social licence to operate: Social acceptability and resource development in Latin America. *The Canadian Mining and Metallurgical Bulletin* (Volume 93, Number 1037): 49–52; Thomson, I. and Joyce, S. 2008. The social licence to operate: What it is and why is seems so hard to obtain. *Proceedings of the 2008 Prospectors and Developers Association of Canada Convention* (Toronto: Prospectors and Developers Association of Canada); Thomson, I. and Boutilier, R. 2011. The Social licence to operate. In *SME Mining Engineering Handbook* (Denver, CO: Society for Mining, Metallurgy, and Exploration); Boutilier, R.G. and Thomson, I. 2011. Modelling and measuring the SLO. Invited paper presented at seminar entitled 'The Social Licence to Operate', Centre for Social Responsibility in Mining, University of Queensland, Brisbane, 15 July. Available from: **http://www.socialicence.com/publications/Modelling%20and%20Measuring%20the%20SLO.pdf** (accessed 27 July 2012).

3. Adler, P. and Kwon, S.-W. 2002. Social capital: Prospects for a new concept. *Academy of Management Review* (Volume 27, Number 10): 27–40.

4. Donaldson, T. and Dunfee, T. 2004. Towards a unified concept of business ethics: Integrative social contracts theory. *Academy of Management Review* (Volume 19, Number 2): 252–284.

5. Kytle, B. and Ruggie, J.G. 2005. Corporate social responsibility as risk management: A model for multinationals. Corporate Social Responsibility Initiative Working Paper Number 10, John F. Kennedy School of Government, Harvard University, Cambridge, MA.

6. Boutilier, R., Black, L. and Thomson, I. 2012. From metaphor to management tool – How the social licence to operate can stabilise the socio-political environment for business. *Proceedings of the International Mine Management Conference,* AusIMM, 21 November.

7. See **http://www.lockthegate.org.au/**

8. Stevens, M., Daley, G. and Priest, M. 2012. Revealed: Coal under green attack. *The Australian Financial Review,* 6 March.

9. Davis, R. and Franks, D. 2011. The costs of conflict with local communities in the extractive industry. Presented at the First International Seminar on Social Responsibility in Mining, Santiago, Chile, 19–21 October.

10. From *Keeping Good Company* (Volume 61, Number 7), the national journal of the Chartered Secretaries of Australia.

11. Inglehart, R. 2000. Globalization and postmodern values. *The Washington Quarterly* (Volume 23, Number 1): 215–228.

12. Boutilier, R., Black, L. and Thomson, I. 2012. From metaphor to management tool – How the social licence to operate can stabilise the socio-political environment for business. *Proceedings of the International Mine Management Conference,* AusIMM, 21 November.

13. ACCSR. 2011. *Upper Hunter Mining Dialogue Report on the Stakeholder Survey for the NSW Minerals Council.* April. Available from **www.accsr.com.au** and **www.nswmin.com.au**.

14. UCI-Net.

15. Teece, D.J., Pisano, G. and Shuen, A. 1997. Dynamic capabilities and strategic management. *Strategic Management Journal* (Volume 18, Number 7): 509–533.

16. Work conducted using this method includes approximately 60 projects completed by ACCSR, Robert Boutilier and Associates and Stakeholder360.com.

17. **http://www.accsr.com.au/html/casestudies1.html**.

18. These questions are drawn from the Stakeholder 360 methodology described in Boutilier, R.G. 2009. Stakeholder politics. In *Stakeholder Politics: Social Capital, Sustainable Development and the Corporation* (Sheffield: Greenleaf).

19. Paulhus, D.L. 1991. Measurement and control of response bias. In J.P. Robinson, P.R. Shaver and L.S. Wrightsman (eds) *Measures of Personality and Social Psychology Attitudes*, Vol. 1, pp. 17–59 (San Diego, CA: Academic Press Inc., Harcourt Brace Jovanovich Publishers).

20. Bainton, N. 2011. Customary dispute handing processes at the Lihir Gold Mine, Papua New Guinea. Paper presented at the Pacific Mining conference, Noumea, November.

21. Disclosure: ACCSR has provided consultancy services to the BMA Local Buying Program.

22. 2011 Census, Australian Bureau of Statistics.

23. World Coal Institute, http://www.worldcoal.org/resources/case-studies/community-investment-programme/ (accessed 7 July 2013).

24. For example, Jacques, O. 2013. BMA attacked for 'ignoring' region's needs. *Fraser Coast Chronicle*, 23 May (accessed 7 July 2013).

25. See http://c-res.com.au/

26. Refers to the Australian financial year runs from 1 July to 30 June. Information sourced from BMA Local Buying Program Quarterly Update YTD March 2013, http://c-res.com.au/ (accessed 7 July 2013).

27. See: http://www.nswmin.com.au/Policy-and-Advocacy/People-and-Communities/Upper-Hunter-Mining-Dialogue/Upper-Hunter-Mining-Dialogue/default.aspx

28. Australian Broadcasting Corporation, 2010. A dirty business. *Four Corners*, 12 April.

29. The public report of the research is available at: http://www.accsr.com.au/html/news.html.

30. Ruggie, J.G. 2013. *Just Business – Multinational Corporations and Human Rights* (New York: W.W. Norton & Company).

31. See **www.theiirc.org**.

....